Santas and Snowmen

Carvings for Christmas

by Tina Toney

Fox Chapel Publishing Co Inc.

Box 7948
Lancaster, PA 17604

DL

Publisher: Alan Giagnocavo
Project Editor: Ayleen Stellhorn
Desktop Specialist: Robert Altland, Altland Design
Cover Photography: Bob Polett, VMI Communications
Step-by-Step Photography: Marvin W. Pierson

ISBN # 1–56523–083–3

To order your copy of this book,
please send check or money order
for $12.95 plus $2.50 shipping to:
Fox Chapel Book Orders
Box 7948
Lancaster, PA 17604–7948

Try your favorite book supplier first!

Acknowledgements

The folks at Plum Fun have been very supportive of my endeavors over the years with helpful suggestions and unending encouragement. A special thank you to the Cole family.

I want to thank my family and friends for their encouragement. My students, my great instructors and my photographer Marvin Pierson. —*Tina Toney*

Table of Contents

Introduction

This book contains patterns and instructions for making 14 Santas and Snowmen. I've also included a step-by-step demonstration on how to carve and paint a Santa. Each piece is carved from commercially available wood products. The Santas and Snowmen on pages 1–13 are carved from sugar pine wood turnings; the ornaments and jewelry are carved from pre-shaped wooden pieces. Some extra components, such as flower pots and dowels, are required for several of the projects and are easily obtained at your local craft store.

A visit to your local craft store can lead to a bonanza of new ideas. Check out the small, shaped, hardwood pieces so popular these days. The bird shapes are easily incorporated with a wood carving. Paint one like a cardinal and add to the Tree-Topped Snowman on page 10. Try different types of glitter sealers. Glue colored jewels to the trees or add snow-like texture mediums to the boughs. The possibilities are endless, so let your imagination go.

Acrylic paints are manufactured by a number of fine companies and are readily available at craft stores. Look through the conversion charts supplied by the various acrylic paint manufacturers; maybe you already have another company's substitute in your supply.

Above all, put safety first while you work through the projects in this book and during your carving in general. Use a glove to protect the hand that holds the carving, keep your tools sharp and avoid as many distractions as possible while you are carving.

Enjoy!—*Tina Toney*

Santas and Snowmen

on Sugar Pine Turnings

Sugar pine, also known as Western white pine, grows throughout the Pacific Northwest states and Canada and is highly sought after by relief and figure carvers. In this book, I've carved sugar pine wood turnings into a number of Santas and snowmen.

A word of caution before you begin your search for sugar pine wood turnings. Not all turnings are sugar pine! Many more turnings are from hardwoods such as birch, maple and ash. These are not suitable for woodcarving. Ask your craft store to order pine turnings from the manufacturer or distributor located in the source section on page 2.

Sugar pine is a light straw color with occasional pink streaking. It will vary in weight from one turning to another. A general rule of thumb is to pick a lighter weight and lighter colored piece to acquire the softer turning. This doesn't always hold true, and any stubborn piece may be wrapped in wet paper towels, inserted in a plastic zip bag and stored in the refrigerator to soften and keep between carving sessions. When the carving is completed, allow it to dry slowly and thoroughly. Remove raised grain with 400-grit sandpaper or a wadded-up brown grocery bag prior to painting and finishing.

Tools and Other Items of Necessity

I have many tools and I love to use them. That is not to say you have to acquire every tool that comes down the pike. You can carve these projects with fewer tools. However, some tools just fit better into certain places. Here's the key issue for me. Will a chisel fit the area being carved better than a knife? If yes, don't be afraid to use it instead.

My philosophy about tools? Acquire good quality tools with enough variety to allow you to carve using the least amount of effort. However, you must keep the tools sharp, for with a dull tool, more effort is expended with less control. There are many fine books available about sharpening. Check out a book from the library or, if you know someone that sharpens well, ask them to teach you.

To carve the projects in this book you'll need the following tools.

Figure 1, top row, from left to right
>   #3 x 1/2" fishtail
>   3/8" u-gouge from a standard set of palm chisels
>   #7 x 1/4" u-gouge
>   1/8" u-gouge from a standard set of palm chisels
>   #11 x 1/8" u-gouge
>   #11 x 1/16" u-gouge

Figure 1 A sampling of the tools needed to carve Santas and Snowmen.

    Model Master Hobby Knife
    Testor's blades
    Small v-tool from a mini-palm chisel set
    Another standard size set
    Bench knife

I also keep the following items on hand: a strop, glue for quick repairs, thumb guards, a hard Arkansas slip stone, some two-part putty and a pencil and eraser. One of the most important items to have is a wood carving glove. Buy a good quality fish filet glove or meat cutter's glove. However, never rely on it solely to protect the hand in which you hold your work. Another neat product available at feed stores is horse wrap, which can be used to pre-wrap thumbs and fingers. One final necessary item is a piece of non-slip mat to lay on your work surface. One such mat available is a rubber router mat, my favorite. (You will notice that I am wearing a support glove on my carving hand. It is especially useful for arthritic hands.)

Some Notes on Wood Burning
Once you are finished carving your Santa or Snowman, you

Sources for materials used by Tina Toney

Plum Fun Wood Products
5427 SE 72nd Avenue
Portland, OR 97206
(503) 777–3511, (503) 777–1126 FAX
Supplier of sugar pine wood turnings and shaped ornaments.

Stan Brown's Arts & Crafts, Inc.
13435 NE Whitaker Way
Portland, OR 97230
1–800–547–553 (phone orders), (503) 252–9508 FAX
Wholesale supplier of turnings, paints and mediums.

Trewax Floor Paste Wax
Available through Ace, TrueValue and other hardware stores as well as Target, K-Mart and Wal-Mart. If your local hardware store does not carry Trewax, you can ask for a special order. Trewax Floor Paste Wax is manufactured by Chemfax. Consumer Service: 1–800–243–6329.

---

may want to add additional details to your piece with a wood burner. I have used a wood burner to add wrinkles around the knuckles, fingernails and stitches to the teddy bear with the Tree-Topped Santa on page 12. Other details on the Santas and snowmen presented in this book can be added at your discretion.

To add details with a cool burn, set the wood burner to the lowest setting that provides a light burn color. Now you may cool burn, with a delicate touch, any number of details.

If you do not have a wood burner, try using your tools to create various effects. For example, you may add stitches to the teddy bear by using the point of a blade, incised a regular intervals to simulate stitches. Antiquing with wax later will allow the finger separations to show.

Optional Power Texturing
Another way to add details to your finished carving is to use a power tool fitted with a round texture stone, round diamond carver or any tip that will create a dimple. Hold the handpiece as you would a pencil, pressing the tip against the wood to dimple it. Proceed over the surface with a random pattern and varied pressure. Fill the area completely, not leaving any spaces between the dimples as they appear unsightly after you paint and antique your piece.

If your carving is fuzzy, try various higher speed increments or different tips. Should it still fuzz, continue to carve until the fur is completed. Several methods will remove this fuzzing. First, lightly brush the fur with a small wooden handled brass brush (available at most hardware stores). Second, a clean green tough pad lightly brushed across the carving has been known to work. Third, use a grocery bag to rub the area. Use fine sandpaper only as a last resort.

If you do not have a power tool, use a small u-gouge to dig dimples into the fur trim. Don't leave any flat areas between gouge marks, as this too will leave an unsightly appearance upon finishing.

Painting
The carving projects in this book have been painted using acrylic craft paints and mediums. I prefer using acrylic for it is non-toxic, odorless and fast drying. The mediums used will help you to control the paints for a longer period of time and aid in its application.

Another reminder, don't apply too much paint. If the paint seems to be too thick, thin it with several drops of flow medium instead of clean water.

Use water plus a drop or two of flow medium to thin the paint for the washes where indicated in the instructions for each project.

On very low humidity days, acrylic paint, without an additive, will dry too quickly, causing the project to appear plastic-like as subsequent layers are applied. If you live in an area where the humidity is very low, add a few drops of the flow medium to the fresh water receptacle. Regardless of weather, always use a flow medium in the fresh water.

On very high humidity days, the acrylic paint nearly refuses to dry. To help it to dry faster, use a hair dryer set on low, held away from the carving. Holding the dryer close to the work can cause the paint to dry too quickly producing bubbles and ugly spots.

On some pieces I have used a permanent pen for eye details and other indicated places. Some permanent pens' lines may smear when you apply the brush-on satin finish. To eliminate smearing, I used light misting of spray satin finish on several pieces to seal the ink details. When using sprays, work in well-ventilated areas.

Antiquing

Several methods of antiquing are used in this book. Some pieces have two methods of antiquing combined, and in some cases, I painted areas and antiqued them before going on to paint other areas. This a somewhat tedious way to go about things, but the results are extremely rewarding. *Father Christmas* is completed in this manner.

One antique method involved uses a paint color plus an antiquing medium, applying with a brush then wiping it off with a lint-free cloth to the desired effect. Follow the manufacturer's instructions for drying time.

The other method of antique is to apply a colored paste wax, followed immediately with clear paste wax to remove the excess color. Soft lint-free clothes (old cotton T-shirts are a good example) work best for waxes. Apply wax in deeper areas with soft tooth brushes. Buffing with soft clots or brushes brings up a nice patina.

I have used Trewax Floor Paste Wax in Clear and Indian Sand throughout this book. Follow the manufacturer's instructions noting the drying time. When using it as an antique, work quickly, applying the colored wax with a brush and cloth. Immediately apply the clear wax using a clean soft cloth, pulling the colored wax off until satisfied with the end results. Use a clean toothbrush loaded with clear for deeper areas. Should you remove too much wax in an area, quickly go back with the color and repeat the process. I allow less than four minutes to pass before I buff the finish to a shine.

Reminder: The unsealed wood surface acts like a sponge. To apply an antique, even to a painted surface, would result in a messy face on your Santa. Where end grain is exposed, the wood will wick the antique. As a result, Santa's forehead and nose become dirty and his clothing takes on a dirty appearance. Incidentally, this kind of mess is hardly repairable unless you cover it with gesso and begin again. The moral: Seal the wood carving adequately.

As you progress through the painting steps in the demonstration section of this book, you will begin to understand what each product's advantages are as well as when and why they are applied.

Turning Patterns

Before you attempt to draw the pattern, you must halve and quarter the turning. Locate the center arch of the growth rings from top to bottom on one side for the face area. Continue straight over and down the opposite side to halve the turning, front to back. Repeat this process at a 90-degree angle to the center-line and you have quartered the turning.

For your first measurement, use a clear plastic ruler, measure the distance on the quarter line from the bottom of the turning to the top of the shoulder.

Set the turning on a shelf at eye level, measure from the shelf up to the required measurement and mark. This requires that you not bend the ruler around the turning but look through the plastic ruler to mark. Lightly pencil in the pattern lines as you repeat this process at all intersections where pattern liens and quarter lines met. Use the quarter lines and lines at the top and bottom of the pattern for all other measurements. Should you feel a need for more reference points, locate the half-way point around the turning and on the pattern.

If you prefer to transfer the pattern using graphite paper, trace the pattern onto individual pieces of tracing paper. Then transfer at the quarter sections one at a time. This method requires some drawing to join one area to another.

Tall Santa with Teddy Bear

MATERIALS

Turning: Sugar pine wood turning (TS120 Plum Fun Wood Products)

Paints: White, Off White, Adobe Wash, Bonnie Blue, Black, Medium Flesh, Tomato Spice, Red, Telemark Green, Brown Iron Oxide, Jo Sonja's Rich Gold. a black permanent pen.

Mediums and Finishes: Jo Sonja's Tannin Blocking Sealer, Jo Sonja's Flow Medium, Jo Sonja's Satin Finish Varnish, Krylon #1311 Matte Finish Spray.

Antique: Trewax Floor Paste Wax in Clear and Indian Sand.

PAINTING TIPS

Seal your woodcarving with the tannin blocker. Paint in the following sequence.

Face: Using a small brush, apply flow medium lightly dampening the cheek area. Dip a $1/8$" angular shader in the flow medium to moisten the brush and pass it across a paper towel to remove the excess. Just touching the brush to the edge of the Tomato Spice, drag the brush outward. Lightly pass the brush across the towel, removing any excess. Test on a piece of scrap wood before applying the paint to your carving. Lightly stipple the cheeks and allow the paint to dry. Should you continue to mess with the partially dry cheeks, splotching will result.

Hands: Use Medium Flesh diluted with flow medium washed across the hands to add slight color.

Eyes: White eye area, painted over with Bonnie Blue iris. Black pupil with White highlight. You may outline the upper eyelid with the permanent pen for detail or cool burn the details.

Beard, Hair, Eyebrows: Off White.

Bear: Fur, Brown Iron Oxide. Tongue, Red. Eyes, Black with White highlight.

Candy Cane: Red and White with Black details.

Clothing: The undergarment is Telemark Green, which is a semi-transparent color. Coat is Tomato Spice diluted with flow medium and water; mix with a palette knife until well-blended to form a wash consistency. Test with a $1/2$" or larger angular shader. Load the brush with the wash and swish it across a piece of newspaper. You should be able to read the print.

Apply the wash with long even strokes, reloading as necessary to achieve an overall color. Allow to dry. Always allow the layers to dry completely before evaluating. Should your Santa's clothing seem too light, apply a second thin wash. The fur trim is Adobe Wash. Rich Gold accent bands on the clothing.

Note: Utmost control must be exercised during the painting of the clothing. Do not allow the wash colors to contaminate adjacent areas.

Sealer: Lightly mist Krylon #1311 to set the ink. Apply Jo Sonja's Satin Finish Varnish.

Antique: When using Trewax, do not allow the wax layers to dry more than three minutes. Carefully avoiding the coat and undergarment, apply Trewax Indian Sand to the rest of the Santa. Using a clean lint-free cloth with Trewax Clear, wipe off excess Indian Sand. For tough areas, use an old, clean tooth brush. Buff to a shine. Repeat with another application of Clear and buff. Waxing the Santa not only gives it a nice patina, but adds an extra protective layer.

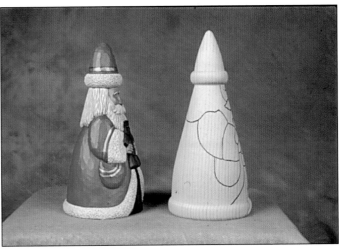

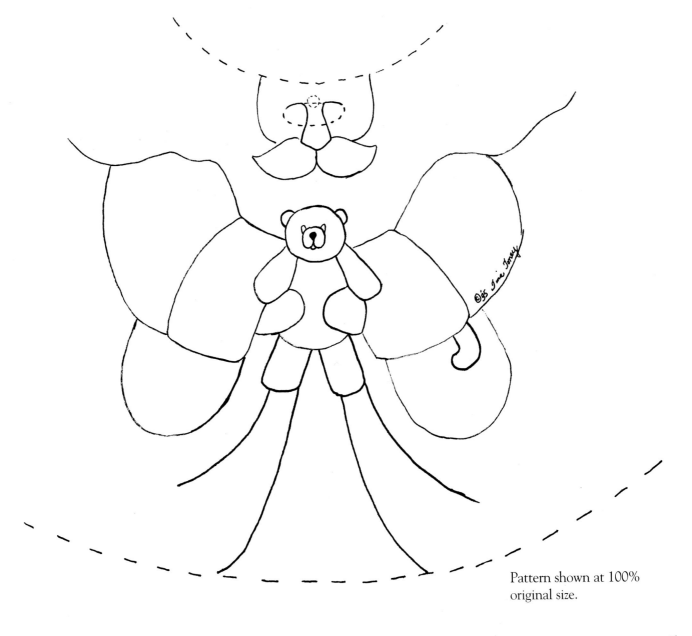

Pattern shown at 100% original size.

Santa with Windswept Beard

MATERIALS

Turning: Jumbo Goose Egg (EG1511, Plum Fun Wood Products)

Paints: Medium Flesh, Dark Flesh, Rouge, White, Antique White, Brown Iron Oxide, Black, Hippo Grey, Sweetheart Blush, Jo Sonja's Rich Gold, black permanent pen.

Mediums and Finishes: White gesso, Jo Sonja's Tannin Blocking Sealer, Jo Sonja's Flow Medium, Jo Sonja's Retarder and Antiquing Medium, Krylon #1311 Matte Finish Spray, Jo Sonja's Satin Finish Varnish

Antique: Trewax Floor Paste Wax in Clear and Indian Sand.

PAINTING TIPS

Apply tannin blocker before painting.

Beard, Hair: Hippo Grey base coat. Antique, cautiously avoiding all surrounding areas, using Jo Sonja's Retarder and Antiquing Medium plus Black. Wipe the black off the high areas. Allow to dry according to the manufacturers instruction. Dry brush across the highest areas with White. Apply white gesso to all remaining white fur trim.

Face: Base coat with Medium Flesh, shade with Dark Flesh and then apply Rouge mixed with Jo Sonja's Flow Medium for the cheek color.

Eyes: White, Brown Iron Oxide, Black. Outline upper lid with permanent pen.

Fur: Antique White.

Clothing: Sweetheart Blush shaded with Black. Mittens, Black. Rich Gold accents on sleeves.

Sealer: Jo Sonja's Satin Finish Varnish.

Antique: Trewax Floor Paste Wax in Indian Sand was applied to the Santa's face and fur trim only. Pull off excess with Clear.

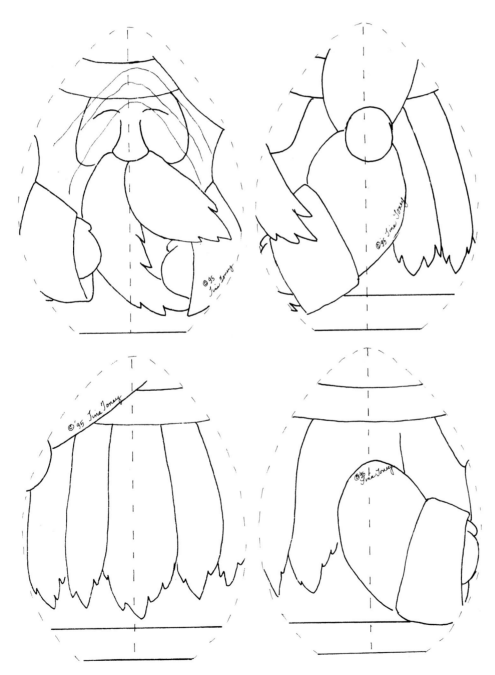

Pattern shown at 68% original size.

Happy Santa

MATERIALS

Turning: Jumbo pear (AP752, Plum Fun Wood Products).

Additional Materials: Large wood flower pot 2 x 1³/4", small finial.

Paints: White, Off White, Antique White, Tomato Spice, Black, Bonnie Blue, Jo Sonja's Rich Gold, Black.

Mediums and Finishes: Jo Sonja's Tannin Blocking Sealer, Jo Sonja's Satin Finish Varnish, Jo Sonja's Flow Medium.

Antique: Trewax Floor Paste Wax in Indian Sand and Clear.

CARVING TIPS

Locate the face on the center of the growth ring arch.

PAINTING TIPS

Sealer: Apply tannin blocker.
Face: This Santa face allows the natural wood to be the flesh color. A thin wash of Tomato Spice plus flow medium was applied sparingly to the cheeks. The eyes are white with a Bonnie Blue iris, a Black pupil and a White highlight.
Hair and Trim: Santa's eyebrows, beard and hair are Off White. The fur trim and finial are Antique White. Accent band, Rich Gold.
Hat: Tomato Spice, shaded with Black.
Antique: Seal the Santa with satin varnish prior to antiquing. Trewax in Indian Sand was applied with a soft toothbrush overall and immediately wiped off with the Clear wax until the desired color was achieved. Do not allow the wax to set more than three minutes before buffing. Apply a second coat of Clear wax for added protection.

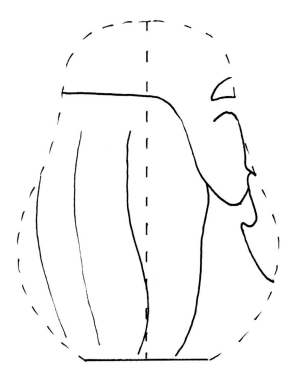
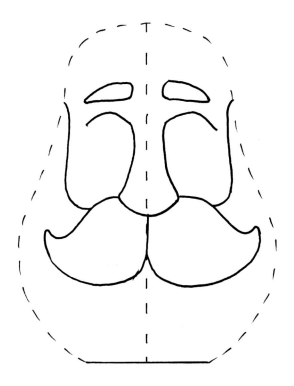

Pattern shown at 100%
original size.

Roly Poly Snowman

MATERIALS

Turning: Sugar pine wood turning (RS121, Plum Fun Wood Products).

Additional Materials: Wood flower pot $1^3/4$" x $1/2$", $3/4$" dowel cap with $1/4$" hole, 1" gluing dowel, $1/4$" wood axle for nose, five-minute epoxy to attach hat.

Paints: White, Fire Red, Pumpkin, Black, Charcoal, Purple, Ultrablue Marine, Deep River, Blue Spruce, Kelly Green, Liquitex Opal Violet, Liquitex Opal Blue, Jo Sonja's Rich Gold.

Mediums and Finishes: Jo Sonja's Tannin Blocking Sealer, Jo Sonja's Retarder and Antiquing Medium, Jo Sonja's Satin Finish Varnish, Delta Sparkle Glaze.

CARVING TIPS

Locate the face on the growth ring arch.

PAINTING TIPS

Seal the snowman with tannin blocker before painting.
Snowman Body: White.
Face: Fire Red dry-brushed on cheeks. Carrot, Pumpkin. Black eyes and mouth.
Belt and Buckle: Belt is Charcoal. Buckle, Purple dry-brushed with opal violet. Buttons are black.
Earmuffs: Ultra Blue shaded with Black and dry-brushed with Opal Blue. Black straps.
Scarf: Deep River shaded with Black, Rich Gold dots and Delta Sparkle Glaze.
Hat: Purple, dry-brushed with Opal Violet. Band, Black

with Rich Gold edges. Purple knob.
Holly: Leaves are Blue Spruce, shaded with Black and Kelly Green highlights. Berries are Fire Red with highlight brush-mixed using Red and White. Black shading on back side of berry. Delta Sparkle Glaze on leaves.
Sealer: Jo Sonja's Satin Finish Varnish.
Antique: Jo Sonja's Retarder and Antiquing Medium plus Black. Brush on, allow to set several minutes, wipe off with a soft lint-free cloth. This mixture dries slowly. A soft cloth may be dabbed in the clear antique medium and used to remove more color if needed. Seal with Jo Sonja's Satin Varnish. Glue all pieces together with five-minute epoxy.

ADDITIONAL PAINTING TIPS

Try painting the body with a base coat of Soldier Blue. Then stipple White over the body with an old brush. Sponge brushes with artist handles are also ideal for this technique.

To antique this version of the Roly Poly Santa, mix Soldier Blue plus antiquing medium, apply it with a brush and wipe off the excess until the desired effect is attained. Allow the snowman to dry thoroughly before applying satin varnish.

Pattern shown at 75% original size.

Tree-Topped Snowman

MATERIALS

Turning: Sugar pine wood turning (TS120, Plum Fun Wood Products).

Additional Materials: Two 1/4" wooden axles for pipe and carrot nose, wooden star 1³/8", wooden match to glue star into tree or a nail glued with five-minute epoxy, drill and drill bit to make hole in star.

Paints: White, Burnt Umber, Forest Green, Dioxazine Purple, Black Green, Pumpkin, Fire Red, Light Yellow, Black, Liquitex Opal Violet, Liquitex Opal Green.

Mediums: Delta Sparkle Glaze, Jo Sonja's Tannin Blocking Sealer, Jo Sonja's Satin Finish Varnish, Jo Sonja's Retarder and Antique Medium.

CARVING TIPS

Carve this snowman with the face on the arch of the growth rings.

Use a small u-gouge to dig a hole at the top of the tree before drilling for placement of the star.

A wooden match can be used to anchor the star to the tree, but a nail will provide a much sturdier attachment.

PAINTING TIPS

Snowman body: White.
Face: Dry-brush Fire Red on the cheeks. Carrot nose is Pumpkin. Pipe is Burnt Umber.
Broom: Burnt Umber with Fire Red dry-brushed across

the straw.
Scarf: Base coat with Forest Green, brush-mix Forest Green with Yellow for lighter areas on the high parts. Shade deeper areas with Black Green. Add Fire Red lines in the scarf for a hint of plaid. Seal with varnish.
Antique: Jo Sonja's Retarder and Antiquing Medium plus Black. Brush on, allow to set several minutes, wipe off with lint-free cloth to desired effect. This mixture dries slowly, allowing ample time to experiment. A soft lint-free cloth may be dabbed in the clear antique medium and used to remove more color if needed. Seal with Jo Sonja's Satin Varnish. Glue all pieces together with five-minute epoxy.

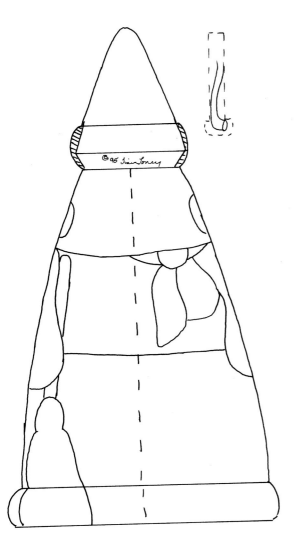

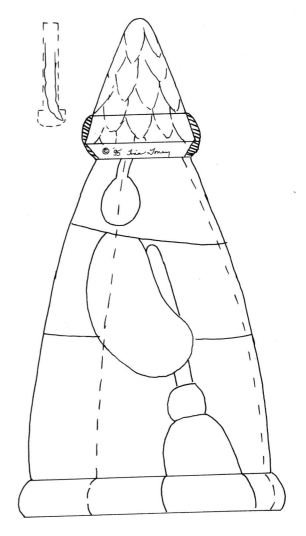

Pattern shown at 75% original size.

Father Christmas

Step-by-Step Demonstration

The following pages include a pattern and step-by-step demonstration on how to carve and paint Father Christmas. Upon completion of the carving process, seal the Santa with tannin blocker.

Divide the turning by halving and quartering using the arch of the growth rings as center for the face alignment.

This project incorporates two methods of antique so pre-paint the hat, coat and cape only. Do not paint the fur trim, hat trim or other areas.

This project incorporates two methods of antique, so pre-paint the hat, coat and cape only. Do not paint the fur trim, hat trim or other areas. You will then be prepared to antique the clothing starting on page 31.

Turning: Sugar pine turning (TS120, Plum Fun Wood Products).

Paints: White, Off White, Antique White, Bonnie Blue, Tomato Spice, Sweetheart Blush, Telemark Green, Black.

Mediums and Finishes: White Gesso, Jo Sonja's Tannin Blocking Sealer, Jo Sonja's Flow Medium, Jo Sonja's Antiquing and Retarding Medium, Jo Sonja's Satin Finish Varnish, Krylon Spray Satin Finish #1311, Trewax Floor Paste in Clear and Indian Sand.

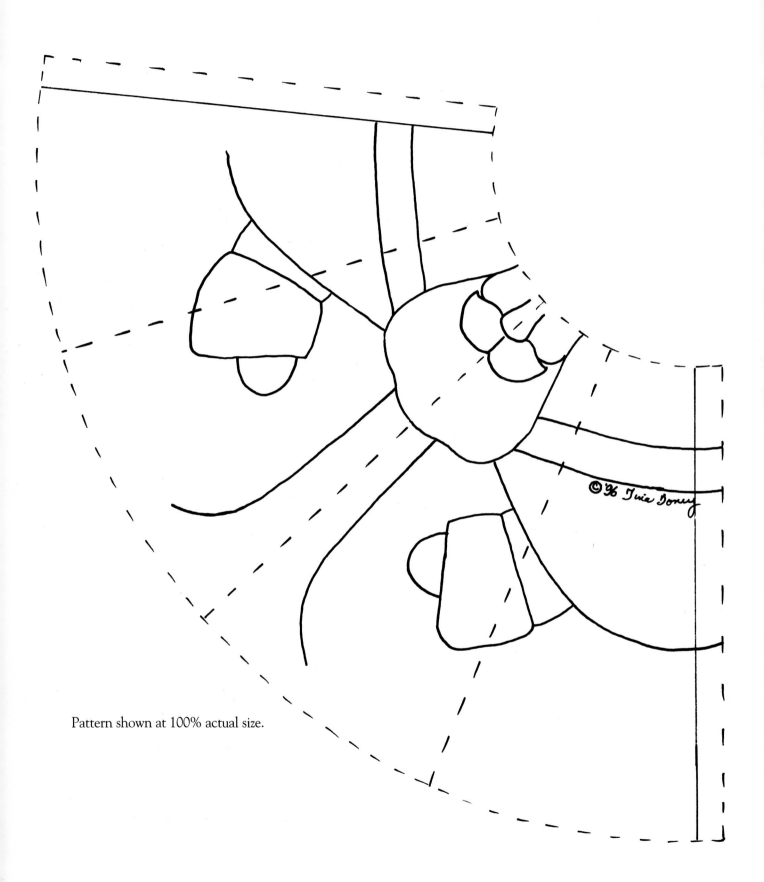

Pattern shown at 100% actual size.

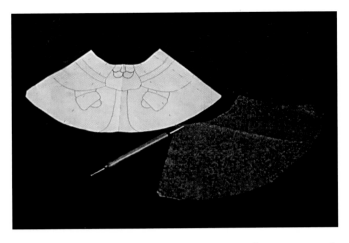

1. You'll need a piece of tracing paper, graphite paper and a pencil to transfer the pattern to the turning. Note: Turnings may vary slightly in size. Compare the pattern with the turning and make any necessary adjustments.

2. Sandwich the graphite paper between the pattern and the wood. Take care to line the centerline of the pattern with the centerline of the turning. Tape the pattern together in the back and trace over the lines with a pencil.

3. The pattern has been transferred with the face located on the center growth arches. Now we're ready to begin carving.

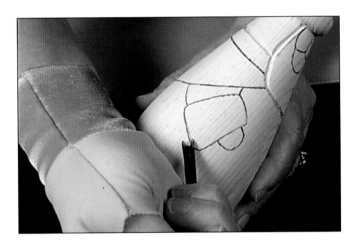

4. Use the v-tool to stop cut behind the arms up to the cape hem. Continue making stop cuts with the v-tool around the beard to the hat trim, between the hair and the top of the collar and on the front fur trim.

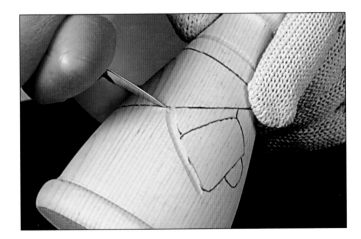

5. With a knife, stop cut straight in at the cape hem.

6. This photo shows all the stop cuts made up to this point.

Carvings for Christmas

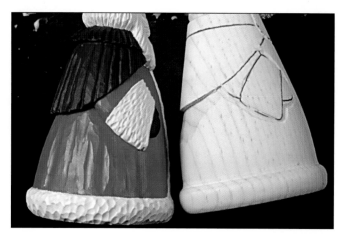

7. Remove wood on the coat up to the cape. Note: The finished Santa's cape will be stair-stepped to the coat.

8. Use the fishtail gouge to remove more wood on the back of the Santa.

9. Taper the cape to the bottom of the collar.

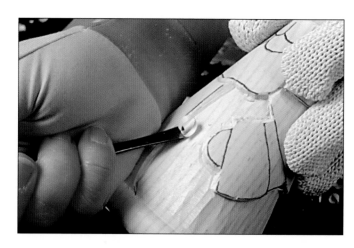

10. Continue to lower the coat adjacent to the front trim.

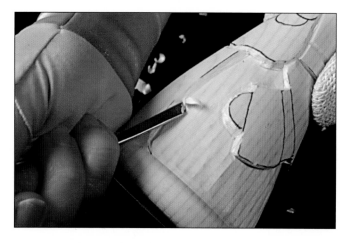

11. Use a skew to lean this area.

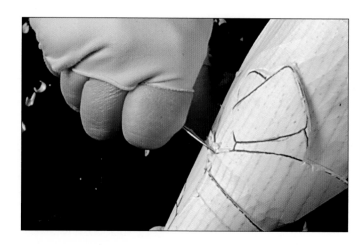

12. Clean up the area more with a bench knife.

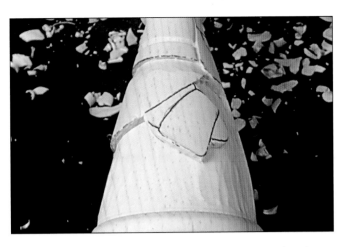

13. This photo shows a view of the levels at the back of the Santa. Note the uneven cape hem. This did get fixed before I finished the project.

14. A side view of the Santa shows the different levels.

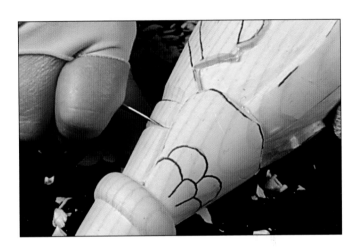

15. Again, a view of the levels from the front.

16. Deepen the stop cut between the hair and the top of the collar.

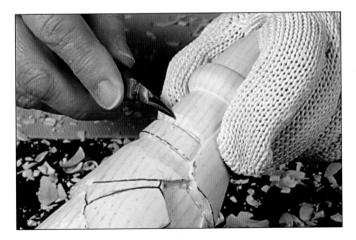

17. Remove wood along the bottom of the hair line to tuck under the collar.

18. Stop cut across the sleeve line.

19. This photo shows the sleeve as it lays under the cape.

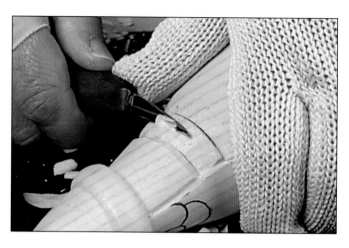

20. Taper the collar to the hair.

21. In this back view of the Santa you can see the various depths of the cuts at this point.

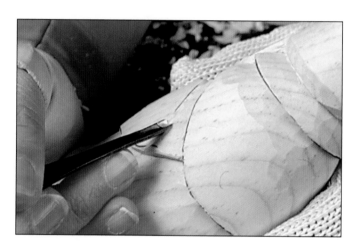

22. V-tool stop cut.

23. Use the chisel turned over to round off the sleeve and the cuffs.

24. Change directions to finish rounding off the cuffs.

25. Make a shallow stop cut between the cuff and the mitten.

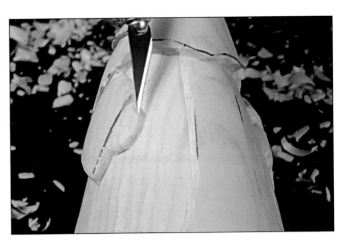

26. Here the mittens have been rounded to satisfaction.

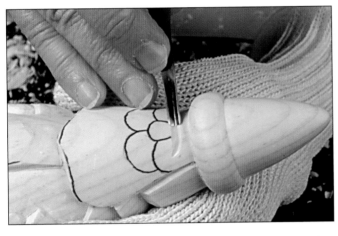

27. Draw the brow arch line, then remove the line with a v-tool.

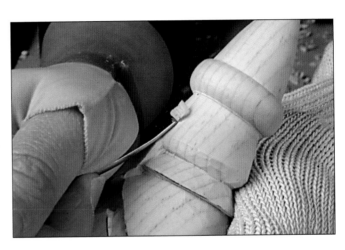

28. Make a straight chisel cut to lower the temples adjacent to the hair.

29. A view of the temple shows the progress up to this point.

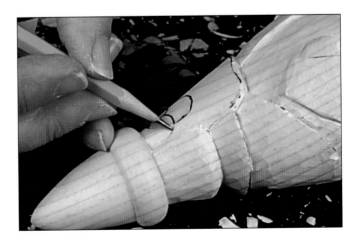

30. Now use a pencil to re-draw the beard lines on the face.

Carvings for Christmas

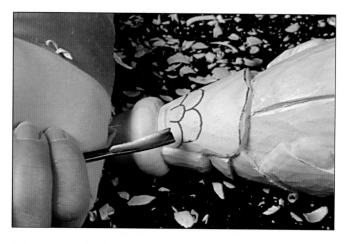

31. Pictured is the u-gouge from the palm chisel set.

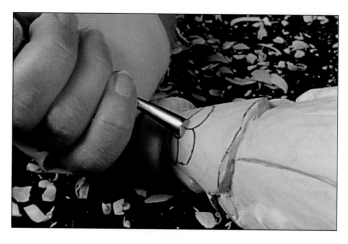

32. Insert the u-gouge straight into the wood on the bottom of the nose, gently rocking it side to side to deepen the cut.

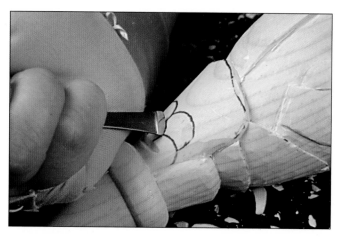

33. Here I am using the ³/₈" gouge to deepen the corner stop cuts.

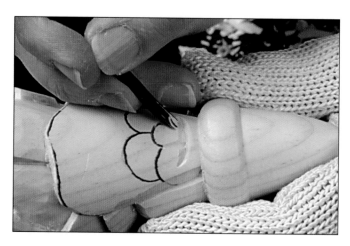

34. Use a v-tool to make the nose lines.

35. Remove the wood from under and around the edge of the nose.

36. Use a v-tool to make the stop cuts around the remainder of the mustache and up to the nose.

37. To allow the nose to protrude, relieve the cheek area, but not too much at this point.

38. A side view of the cheek area shows the depths from a different view.

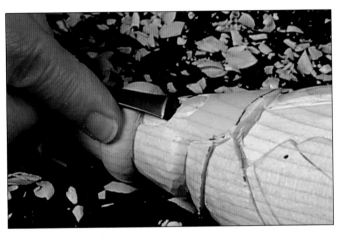

39. Working on the right portion of the face, turn the gouge over. Following the slope of the cheek, insert the gouge and undercut the mustache slightly.

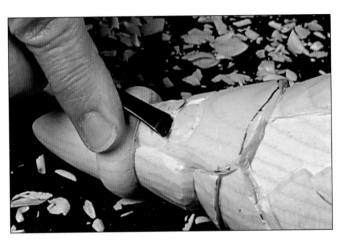

40. Work across the cheek area, following the cheek slope up to the intersection with the nose.

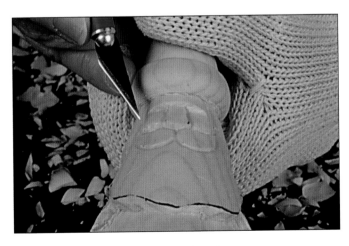

41. Both cheeks are now completed.

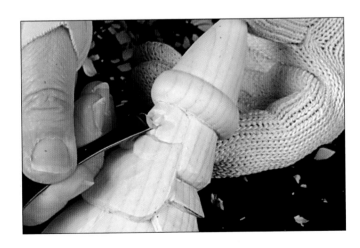

42. Round off the nose, shape the beard and mustache and remove all the original sanded surface on the beard.

43. The beard has now been roughed out and should look like this.

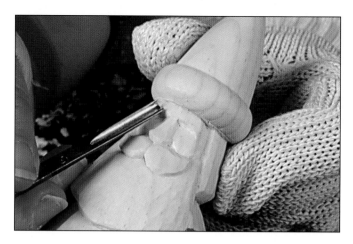

44. Use a small u-gouge to carve the divot between the eyebrows.

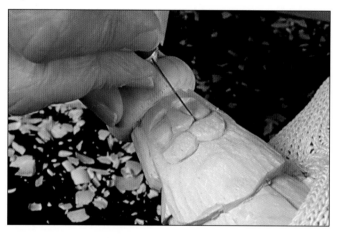

45. Use a knife to shape around the nostril flares and to create a division between them and the cheek.

46. Continue carving a short distance up the nose.

47. Take a break to take a good look at your Santa so far. Is his face shaping up the way you want it to? Make any necessary adjustments before moving on.

48. Draw the eyes on the face with a pencil.

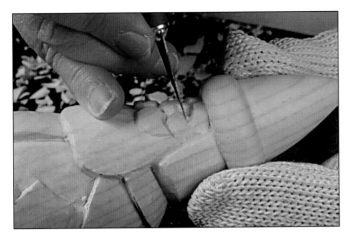

49. Continuing with the knife, make a shallow stop cut on the bottom eyelid and outside of the top eyelid.

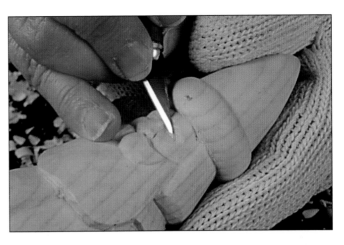

50. Remove the wood at the outside corner of the eyes.

51. Repeat the same procedure on the inside corners of the eyes.

52. Cut the small nostril holes with the knife and draw in the top of the eyebrows for detailing at a later time.

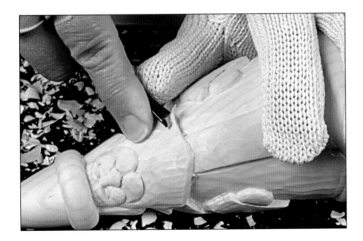

53. Round off the beard.

54. Draw the separation between the thumb and the hand.

55. Make a stop cut by pushing the knife straight into the wood.

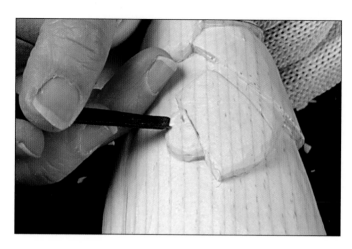

56. V-tool from this point to the stop cut.

57. Finish carve the hand down to the clothing.

58. Use a u-gouge to detail the fur cuffs. Fill in with a random pattern until the cuff no longer has any previously carved surface remaining.

59. Draw a long oval in the sleeve below the hand.

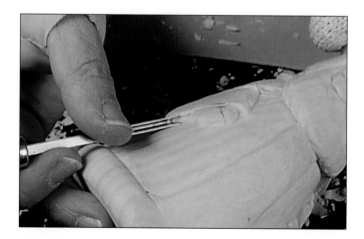

60. Remove a small ditch and finish carve the intersection between the hand and the cuff.

Santas and Snowmen

61. Draw the pleat lines on the cape.

62. Use a large v-tool to carve the pleats.

63. Draw the pleat lines of the collar and use a veiner from the outside edge toward the hair.

64. Collar and cape completed.

65. Texture the hat trim with a small v-tool.

66. Carve the top knot and detail this area in the same manner as the cuff.

67. Shape the fabric folds of the hat with a v-tool and bench knife.

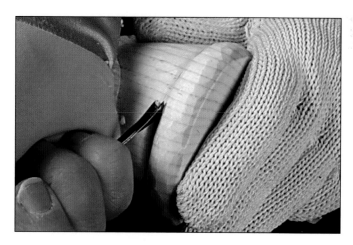

68. On to the coat fur trim... Carve away the original sanded surface. Then use the v-tool around the trim for clean up.

69. Use the skew to level the coat to the trim area. This area is prepped for final details that we'll pick up on later.

70. Draw the curved beard and hair lines as a loose guide for details. The area between these will be filled in with long and short v-gouge details.

71. Start the mustache details with the v-tool in this position. Come back later and detail from this starting position, around the mustache and down to the beard. It may be easier for you to do this step with a knife.

72. Repeat this process for the beard.

28

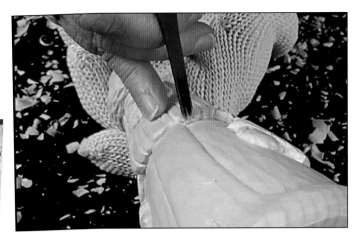

73. Carve down and around the beard to the clothing.

74. Basic beard and mustache.

75. The beard and mustache are completed. Use the knife to remove wood above the top of the eyebrows.

76. Clean up the forehead to the hat.

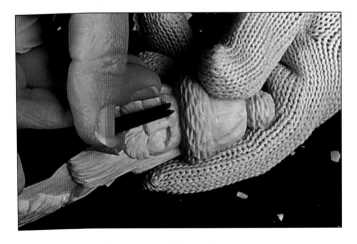

77. Use a v-tool to texture the eyebrows.

78. Draw in the draping areas for the coat and use assorted u-gouges to detail the area.

79. The coat is now completed.

80. Carve the coat front to separate and expose the undergarment.

81. Detail the fur trim with any u-gouge you like. I have used a #7 x 1/4" u-gouge.

82. The carving is now complete.

83. Compare your carving to the side view of the carving in this photo. Make any necessary adjustments.

84. Check the back view of the piece as well before you call your Santa finished.

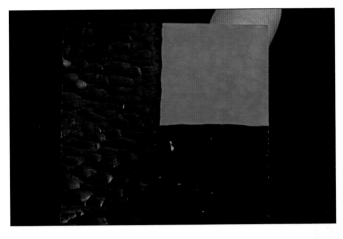

1. The antiquing on the left half of the board has been wiped down once with a dry cloth.

2. Dip a folded cloth into the clear antique. Be careful not to super saturate the cloth.

3. Wipe off more of the antique until you are pleased with the effect.

4. This photo shows the back view of the antiqued Santa.

5. A side view of the antiqued Santa to this point.

6. Close-up of the clothing area. Allow it to dry thoroughly before proceeding.

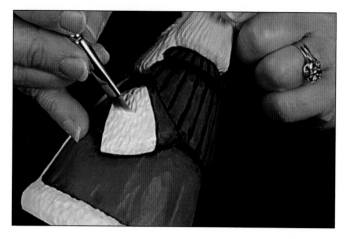

7. Apply gesso to the sleeve trim.

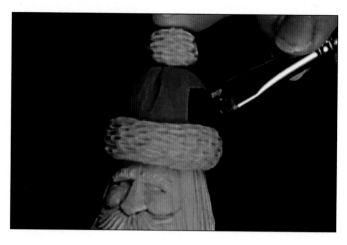

8. Slightly pre-moisten the hat with antique medium for added control.

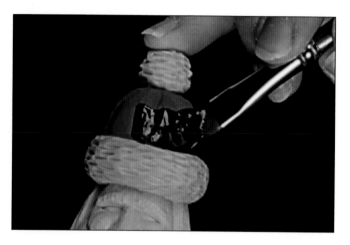

9. Apply antique.

10. Let it dry several minutes.

11. Wipe.

12. Just right.

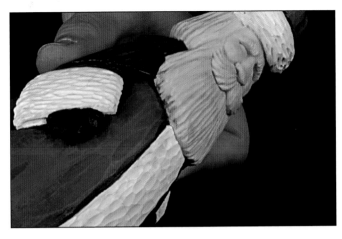

13. View of antiqued front clothing. Allow the antiquing to dry several days before proceeding any further. Gesso hat trim.

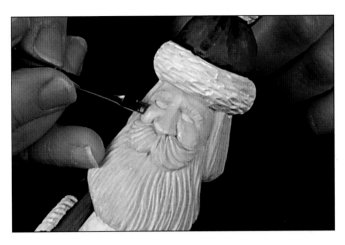

14. Slightly pre-moisten the cheek area with flow medium.

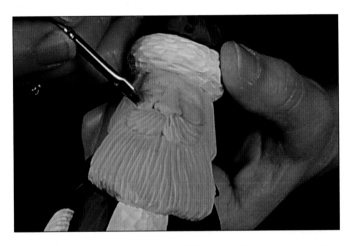

15. Pick up a sparse amount of Tomato Spice paint and drag it across a clean area of the palette to remove any excess paint. Apply it to the cheek area and feather the edges.

16. Cheek color applied.

17. Paint the eyes White.

18. Add a Bonnie Blue iris to each.

19. Paint a Black pupil and dot in a White highlight.

20. Base coat the beard and hair with gesso. When dry paint them with Off White. The under garment is Telemark Green. Paint the clothing fur trim with Antique White.

21. Seal the Santa with Jo Sonja's Satin Finish Varnish now. Apply a second coat to the face. Apply the Indian Sand wax to the face and all white areas with a clean toothbrush and soft cloth. Be careful to avoid the clothing.

22. Immediately pull the colored wax off with a cloth loaded with Clear wax. Do not leave it on for the full five minutes as recommended by the manufacturer. I find I get much better results when antiquing if I work faster.

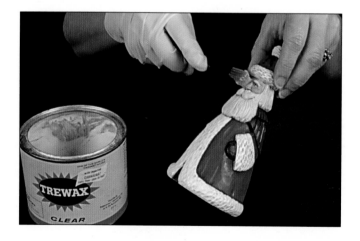

23. A clean toothbrush loaded in Clear wax will pull unwanted wax from more detailed areas. Buff the Santa with a clean soft cloth or brush.

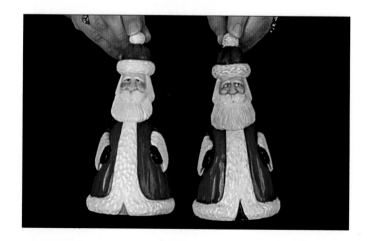

24. Compare one Santa to the other. One lacks antiquing. If you decide not to antique, apply a coat of Clear wax overall, let it set less than three minutes and buff. Apply two coats for added protection.

Santas and Snowmen

Santas and Snowmen

Ornaments and Jewelry

Christmas Ornaments

Relief carving methods are employed for these little gems. The two sided Santa on page 51 may be carved on one side for a necklace or both sides as a tree ornament. All of the pieces in this section can be carved for necklaces, pins, ornaments or kitchen magnets. An idea came to mind recently to mount the finished ornaments onto florist sticks to add to the greenery of Christmas arrangements. The possibilities are endless.

Several of these patterns require tracing to onion skin and then transferring them to the wood with a piece of graphite paper. Most are just as easily drawn.

H Clear white fields represent the highest areas of wood and are the last areas to be carved.

M Start the woodcarving process with these medium areas. Remove a thin layer of wood, but less than you'll remove from the areas marked L.

L On the lower levels, remove even more wood, creating a third level.

D Remove the most wood from these areas.

Roughing Out

Study the drawings closely beforehand and carve to the levels indicated. The back of the blanks have holes used in the manufacturing process, so avoid carving too deeply. Do not carve one area to completion before carving another. Hint: paint the backside of the ornament before carving the project. Refer to the individual ornament directions for suggested colors.

Carve in an orderly overall fashion before the final details are carved. During the rough out carving, stop to examine each area, comparing side to side to reach a balance between the levels. Redraw, as necessary, the center line to aid in your comparison. Make any adjustments prior to the finish carving if detected. Don't get in a hurry!

Rounding Off

When you have completed the rough out, round off the sharp edges of your stop cuts blending between the basic four levels.

Detail Carving

The high areas should be the only surface left to carve at this point. Use a hobby knife with a new blade inserted for the detail carving. The high areas are the original sanded surface of the blank and must be removed. Lay the blade on the wood surface, tilt the back of the blade slightly and remove small chips shaped like fish scales until the surface is completely free of sanded areas. Remove small slivers and rough spots in preparation for painting.

Sealing The Carving

Seal all ornaments with Jo Sonja's Tannin Blocking Sealer before painting. I recommend painting the back side of the carving, especially if you are using it as a piece of jewelry. The painting and antiquing techniques used on the ornaments and jewelry are the same as those used on the sugar pine wood turnings. Turn to page 1 for some tips or to page 15 for a demonstration.

Baldy Santa

MATERIALS

Wood: Tall puffed teardrop (PP485, Plum Fun Wood Products)

Paints: White, Antique White, Black, Country Red, Blush, Bonnie Blue, Medium Flesh, Shading Flesh, Brown Iron Oxide.

Mediums and Finishes: Jo Sonja's Tannin Blocking Sealer, Jo Sonja's Satin Finish Varnish, Jo Sonja's Flow Medium, Jo Sonja's Retarder and Antiquing Medium.

PAINTING TIPS

Seal the Baldy Santa with tannin blocker. Paint the flat side Country Red.

Face: Use Medium Flesh as the base coat the face. Mix flow medium with Shading Flesh. Use on the face around the beard, hairline and beside the nose. Brush-mix the flow medium with Medium Flesh and White to a slightly lighter shade to highlight his bald head. Slightly moisten the cheek area with flow medium and apply Blush to the area, blending at edges where it meets the Medium Flesh.

Eyes: Paint the eye area White with a Bonnie Blue iris, a Black pupil and a White highlight.

Hair and Beard: Antique White.

Clothing: Country Red.

Antique: Mix Brown Iron Oxide and antiquing medium. Apply with a brush and wipe with lint-free cloth to desired effect. Allow to dry and seal with satin varnish.

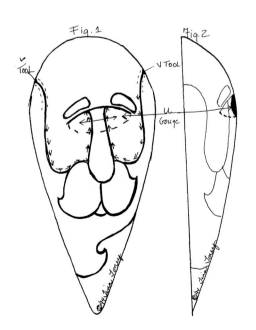

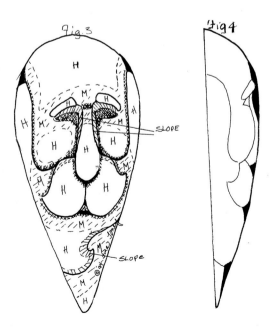

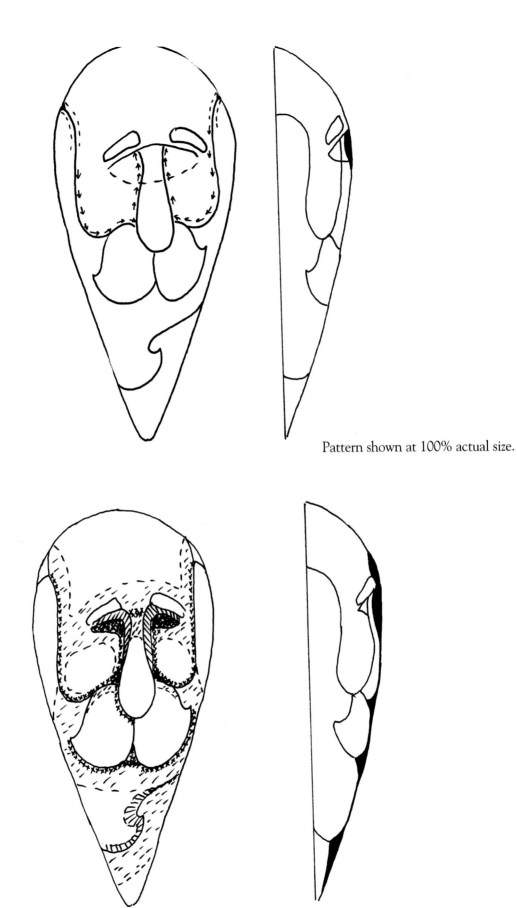

Pattern shown at 100% actual size.

Festive Snowman

MATERIALS

Wood: Tall puffed teardrop (PP485, Plum Fun Wood Product)

Paints: White, Antique White, Black, Blush, Orange, Liberty Blue, Dark Forest, Liquitex Opal Green, Jo Sonja's Rich Gold.

Mediums: Jo Sonja's Tannin Blocking Sealer, Jo Sonja's Satin Finish Varnish, Jo Sonja's Retarder and Antiquing Medium.

PAINTING TIPS

Seal the Festive Snowman with the tannin blocker.

Face: Snowman is painted white. Dry brush Blush onto the cheeks. Orange carrot nose. Black eyes with White highlight. Black outline on edge of lip.

Hat and Scarf: Hat tassel Antique White. Hat and scarf are Dark Forest with Opal Green applied sparingly over the Dark Forest.

Seal with satin varnish.

Antique: Mix Dark Forest and smidgen of Liberty Blue with flow medium. Apply with a brush, let set several minutes before wiping off with lint-free cloth. Allow to dry. Apply Rich Gold dots as shown in illustration. Apply a final coat of varnish.

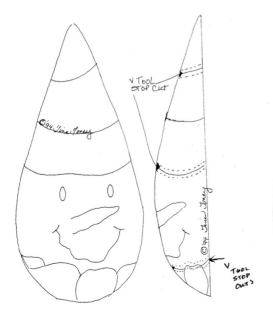

Pattern shown at 100% actual size.

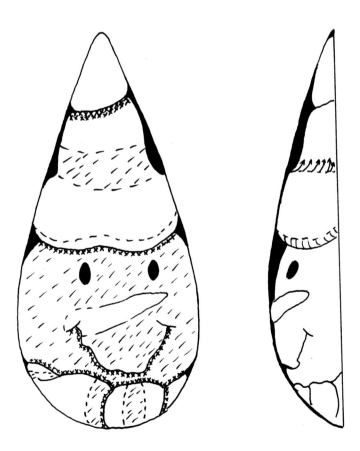

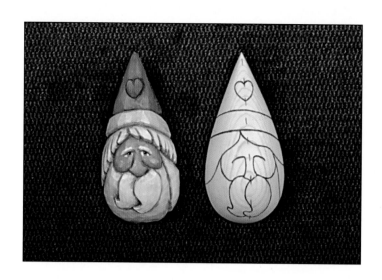

Teardrop Santa

MATERIALS

Wood: Tall puffed teardrop (PP485, Plum Fun Wood Products)

Paints: White, Off-white, Antique White, Black, Country Red, Blush, Bonnie Blue, Medium Flesh, Shading Flesh and Brown Iron Oxide.

Mediums: Jo Sonja's Tannin Blocking Sealer, Jo Sonja's Matte Finish Varnish, Jo Sonja's Flow Medium, Jo Sonja's Retarder and Antiquing Medium.

PAINTING TIPS

Seal the Teardrop Santa with tannin blocker and paint the back Bonnie Blue.

Face and Eyes: Paint the face Medium Flesh and shade with the Shading Flesh in the deeper areas. Using flow medium with the Shading Flesh allows for easier manipulation. With flow medium, slightly moisten the cheek area then apply blush, lightly feathering the edges to blend into surrounding areas. Paint eyes White with a Bonnie Blue iris, a Black pupil and a White highlight.

Hair and Fur Trim: Eyebrows, beard and hair are Off White. Fur trim on hat is Antique White.

Hat: Bonnie blue with Country Red heart. Shade around the heart and above the fur trim with Black plus antiquing medium.

Antique: Mix Brown Iron Oxide and antique medium to antique the Santa's face. Wipe off and seal with satin varnish.

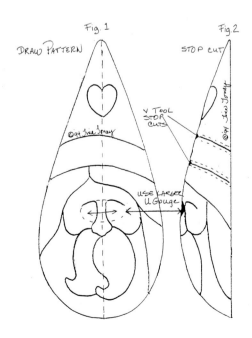

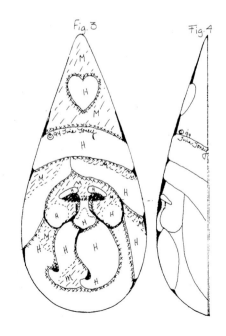

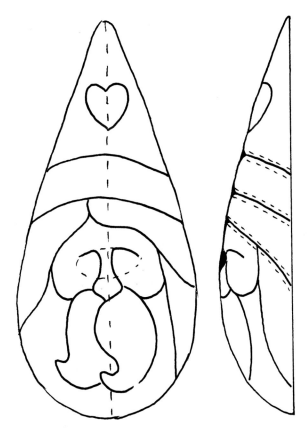

Pattern shown at 100% actual size.

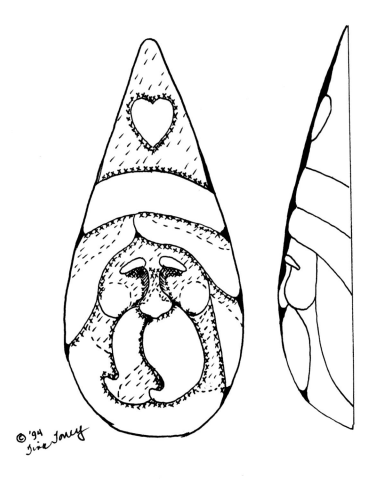

© '94
Jive Toney

Old World Santa

MATERIALS

Wood: Puffed angel shape (PP469, Plum Fun Wood Products)

Paints: White, Antique White, Hippo Grey, Black, Brown Iron Oxide, Dark Forest, Blush, Medium Flesh, Shading Flesh, Liquitex Opalescents Opal Green, Jo Sonja's Rich Gold.

Mediums: Jo Sonja's Flow Medium, Jo Sonja's Tannin Blocking Sealer, Jo Sonja's Satin Finish Varnish, Jo Sonja's Retarder and Antiquing Medium.

PAINTING TIPS
Seal the Old World Santa with tannin blocker and base coat the back of the ornament with Dark Forest.

Face and Eyes: Paint the face with Medium Flesh. Brush-mix flow medium with Shading Flesh and shade around the face. Dry-brush Blush onto the cheek area. Paint the eyes White, with a Brown Iron Oxide iris, a Black pupil and a White highlight.

Hair and Beard: Hippo Grey for eyebrows, hair and beard. Dry brush White across the texture lines. Allow Grey to show from lower areas.

Clothing: Hat trim is Antique White. Hat, Dark Forest with Opal Green dry-brushed sparingly. Shade above the fur band and below tassel with Black. Seal with satin varnish.

Antique: Mix antiquing medium and Brown Iron Oxide, apply with brush, wipe off with lint-free cloth. Allow to dry. Apply Rich Gold accents, then seal with satin finish varnish.

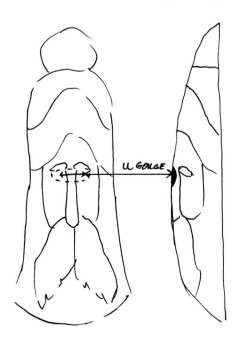

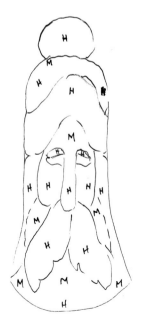

Pattern shown at 100% actual size.

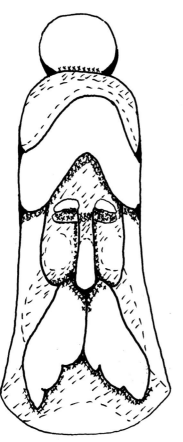

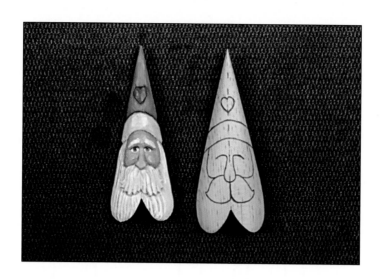

Primitive Santa

MATERIALS

Wood: Small puffed primitive heart or large puffed primitive heart (PP466 or PP467, Plum Fun Wood Products).

Paints: White, Off White, Antique White, Black, Country Red, Blush, Bonnie Blue, Medium Flesh, Shading Flesh, Brown Iron Oxide.

Mediums: Jo Sonja's Tannin Blocking Sealer, Jo Sonja's Satin Finish Varnish and Jo Sonja's Retarder and Antiquing Medium.

PAINTING TIPS
Seal the ornament with tannin blocker and paint the back with Bonnie Blue.

Face and Eyes: Medium Flesh over face shaded with Shading Flesh. Dry-brush Blush across the cheeks. Eyes are painted White with a Bonnie Blue iris, Black for the pupil and a White highlight.

Hair and Fur Trim: Off White for hair and beard. Antique White for trim.

Hat: Hat is Bonnie Blue with Country Red heart. Shade around the heart and fur trim with Black.

Antique: Mix Brown Iron Oxide with antiquing medium. Apply to Santa with brush, wipe off to desired effect with lint-free cloth. Allow to dry and seal with satin varnish.

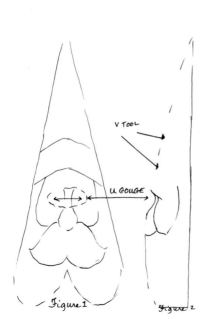

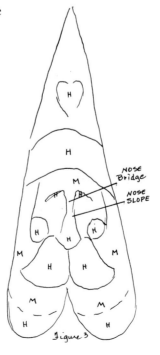

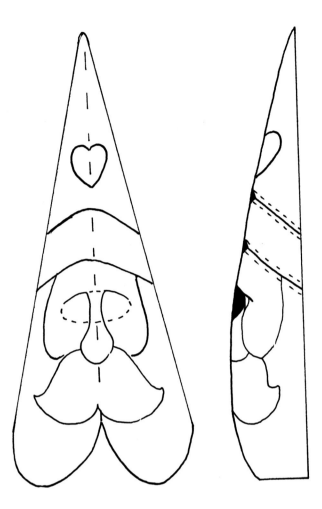

Pattern shown at 100% actual size.

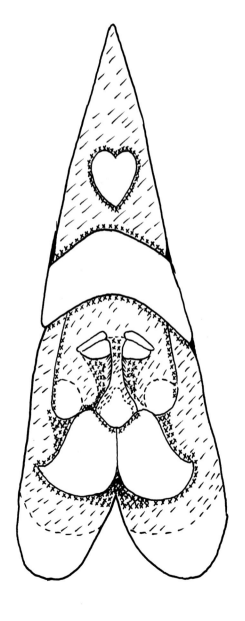

Puffed Santa Pin

MATERIALS

Wood: Santa Puffed Shape (PP470, Plum Fun Wood Products)

Paints: White, Off White, Antique White, Black, Country Red, Blush, Deep River, Bonnie Blue, Medium Flesh, Shading Flesh, Brown Iron Oxide.

Mediums: Jo Sonja's Tannin Blocking Sealer, Jo Sonja's Satin Finish Varnish, Jo Sonja's Flow Medium, Jo Sonja's Retarder and Antiquing Medium.

PAINTING TIPS

Seal your Santa with tannin blocker, let it dry and paint the back of the project with Deep River.

Face and Eyes: Paint face Medium Flesh, shade around the face with Shading Flesh. Pre-moisten the cheeks with flow medium, apply Blush and feather at the edges to blend. The eyes are White with Bonnie Blue iris, Black pupil and White highlight.

Hair and Beard: Off White, same for eyebrows.

Fur Trim: Antique White.

Hat: Hat is Deep River, ³/₄" Black band. Country Red for the hearts. Squiggle lines at the edge of Black band are Antique White. Use Black to shade around the hat leaving the lighter Deep River to show through. Brush-mix Country Red with Off White to apply to the highlighted areas of the hearts. Hearts are shaded with Black. Seal with satin varnish prior to antiquing.

Antique: Mix antique medium with Brown Iron Oxide. Apply with brush and immediately wipe off with lint-free cloth to desired effect. Dry according to manufacturers instruction before final protective coat of satin varnish.

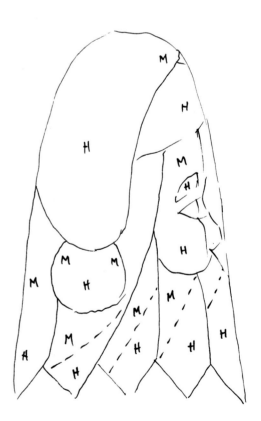

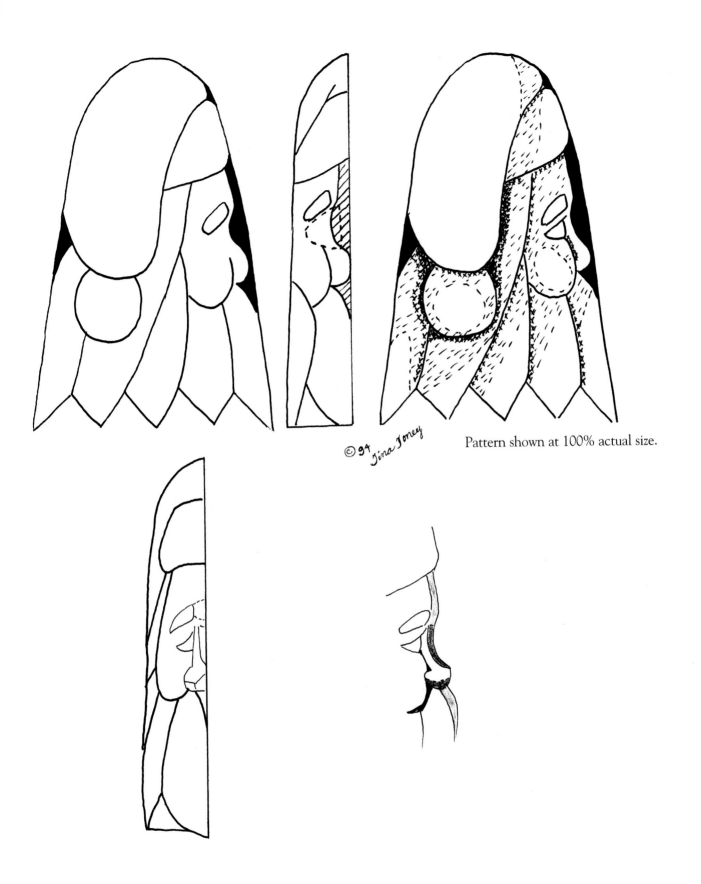

©94 Tina Toney

Pattern shown at 100% actual size.

Puffed Heart Santa Pin

MATERIALS

Wood: Folk Art Heart Shape (PP451, Plum Fun Wood Products)

Paints: White, Off White, Antique White, Bonnie Blue, Black, Sweetheart Blush, Red, Tomato Spice, Adobe Red, Deep River, Kelly Green, Brown Iron Oxide, Rich Gold, black permanent pen.

Mediums: Jo Sonja's Tannin Blocking Sealer, Jo Sonja's Satin Finish Varnish, Jo Sonja's Flow Medium, Jo Sonja's Retarder and Antiquing Medium.

PAINTING TIPS

Seal your Santa with tannin blocker, let dry and paint the back with Deep River.

Face and eyes: Pre-moisten the cheeks with flow medium, apply Blush and feather at the edges to blend. The eyes are White with Bonnie Blue iris, Black pupil and white highlight.

Hair, eyebrows and beard: Off White.

Fur trim: Antique White.

Hat: Hat is Sweetheart Blush, shaded with Black. Band is Tomato Spice shaded with Black. Holly leaves are Deep River with Kelly Green highlights. Use a permanent pen for details and Rich Gold for crosshatching. Paint a four-petal design within the squares with Sweetheart Blush. Add a Rich Gold dot inside the center.

Antique: Avoiding the hat, antique with antique medium mixed with Brown Iron Oxide. Apply with brush and immediately wipe off with lint-free cloth to desired effect. Dry according to manufacturers instruction before final protective coat of satin varnish.

48

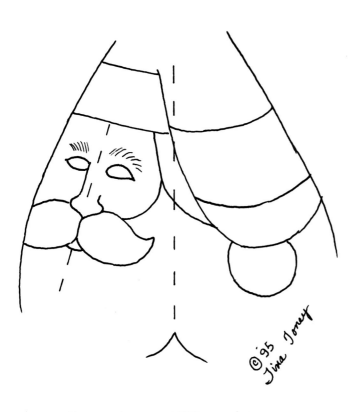

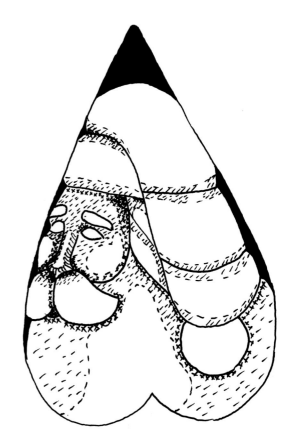

Pattern shown at 100% actual size.

Copy pattern to tracing paper and transfer to the wood with graphite paper.

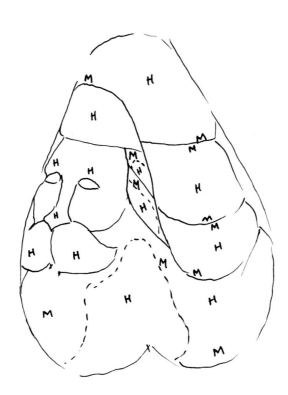

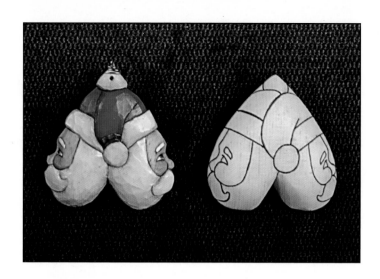

Santa Necklace

MATERIALS

Wood: Small or medium puffed hearts (PH1011 and PH1009, Plum Fun Wood Products)

Paints: White, Off White, Antique White, Blush, Red, Black, Bonnie Blue, Brown Iron Oxide, Jo Sonja's Rich Gold, black permanent pen.

Mediums: Jo Sonja's Tannin Blocking Sealer, Jo Sonja's Satin Finish Varnish, Jo Sonja's Flow Medium, Jo Sonja's Retarder and Antiquing Medium, Krylon #1311 Matte Finish Spray.

PAINTING TIPS

Seal your necklace with the tannin blocker prior to painting. If you have carved a one-sided Santa, paint the back with Red.

Face and Eyes: The Santa's face has the natural wood as the flesh color. Pre-wet the cheek area with flow medium sparingly. Dry-brush Blush onto the cheeks, allow it to dry before adding other layers. The eye area is White with a Bonnie Blue iris, Black pupil and White highlight.

Hair and Fur: The beard, hair and eyebrows are Off White. The fur trim of the hat is Antique White.

Hat: The hat is Red. Note: The accent band has been wood burned as well as around the eyes and other features of this Santa. The permanent pen can be substituted for the eye and outline of the gold band details.

Antique: Prior to antiquing, lightly mist with Krylon #1311 to set the ink. Mix Brown Iron Oxide and antiquing medium, apply with a brush, wipe away until

satisfied with its appearance. Allow to dry according to manufacturer's directions and seal with a final application of satin varnish. Clear Trewax Floor Paste Wax adds extra color depth and protection of the surface.

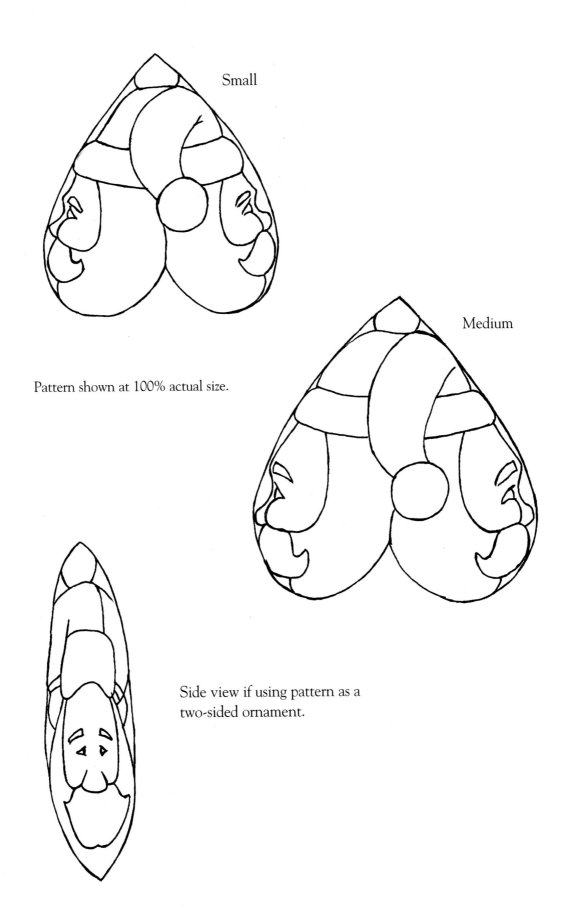

Small

Medium

Pattern shown at 100% actual size.

Side view if using pattern as a
two-sided ornament.